Quiltscapes

Rebecca Barker

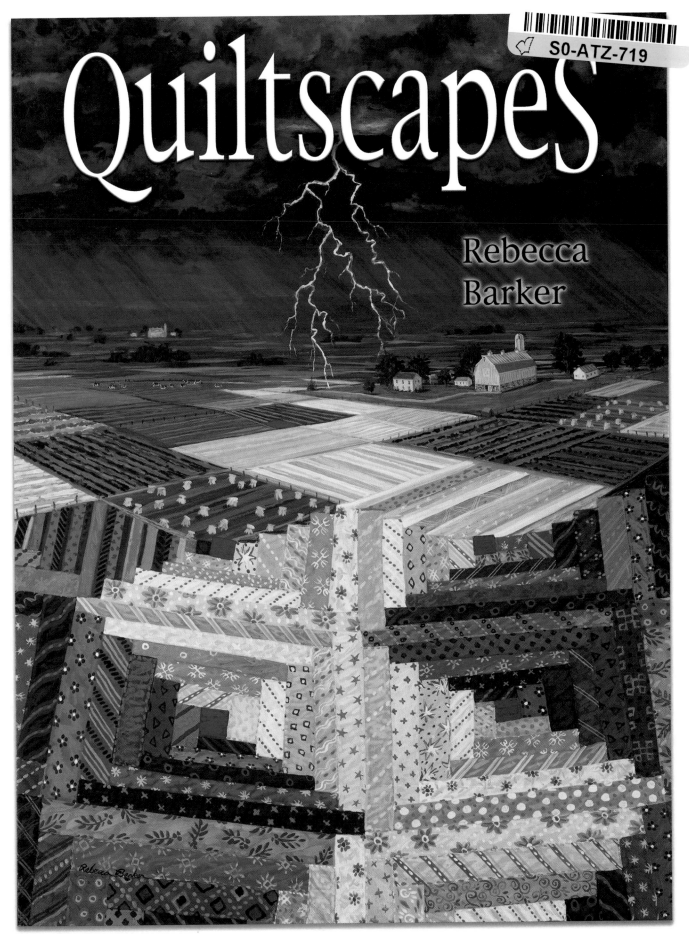

American Quilter's Society

P. O. Box 3290 • Paducah, KY 42002-3290

www.AQSquilt.com

Located in Paducah, Kentucky, the American Quilter's Society (AQS) is dedicated to promoting the accomplishments of today's quilters. Through its publications and events, AQS strives to honor today's quiltmakers and their work and to inspire future creativity and innovation in quiltmaking.

EDITOR: BARBARA SMITH

GRAPHIC DESIGN: ELAINE WILSON

COVER DESIGN: MICHAEL BUCKINGHAM

Library of Congress Cataloging-in-Publication Data
Barker, Rebecca, 1953–
    Quiltscapes / by Rebecca Barker
        p. cm.
        ISBN 1-57432-811-5
    1. Patchwork--Patterns. 2. Appliqué--Patterns. 3.
Quilting--Patterns. I. Title.
TT835 .B2665 2003
746.46'041--dc21

                        2002154155

Additional copies of this book may be ordered from the American Quilter's Society, PO Box 3290, Paducah, KY 42002-3290, or online at www.AQSquilt.com.

Copyright © 2003, Rebecca Barker
Licensing Agent: Intermarketing Group

(on the title page)

STREAK OF LIGHTNING

The idea for this painting came to me while I was flying in a jet over the Midwest. This is one of my favorite patterns, and the Log Cabin, in the Streak of Lightning setting, is one of my favorite quilts.

Dedication

With heart-felt thanks to…

My parents, for supporting my choice to be an artist and always being there for me.

My sister, Margaret, for helping me with my writing. She is an inspiration in my life.

Barbara Smith and the American Quilter's Society design department for editing and designing a creative and fun page-turner.

At the Depot

This railroad station is located in Cincinnati, Ohio. I love old buildings, and I think this one is a beauty and perfect for depicting the quilt pattern called AT THE DEPOT.

Butterflies on Nine Patches

My mother liked this painting so much she made a quilt just like it, including embroidered butterflies. These are real butterflies I found in a field identification book.

Contents

Introduction

Rebecca calls her paintings "Quiltscapes" because they depict the titles of old-time quilt patterns. The paintings have a realistic style with an emphasis on color, clarity, and composition. She works on the smooth surface of masonite board, which gives the acrylic paint the three-dimensional look.

For each of the 29 beautiful quilt paintings presented, you will find a pattern of the block or blocks depicted. Rotary cutting measurements are given for those patches that can be rotary cut. Full-sized patterns are provided for those patches that do not lend themselves to rotary cutting. For the appliqué blocks, you will need to add ³⁄₁₆" turn-under allowances to the patch patterns. For the pieced blocks, add ¼" seam allowances.

For your convenience in planning your projects, the pieced blocks are accompanied by yardage charts. You can use these charts to find out how many pieces can be cut from either a fat quarter, for scrap quilts, or a full yard. Five of the pieced blocks are appliqué, and 23 of the blocks are pieced. Try combining like-sized blocks in your quilts for added excitement. Some of the blocks will be quite easy to sew for those who are familiar with basic quiltmaking techniques. Several of the blocks may be quite challenging even for experienced quilters.

Rebecca says, "As an artist, I fully appreciate the composition and design talent it took to create the beautiful quilt patterns. It is my goal to honor the women who created these designs and to teach others the names of the patterns."

Block Patterns

Chickadees on Bridal Wreath

This is a simple but lovely quilt pattern. I have used it in several paintings and with other birds, but I think chickadees are perfect for this pattern because they always seem to have a spouse.

Cardinal on Whig Rose

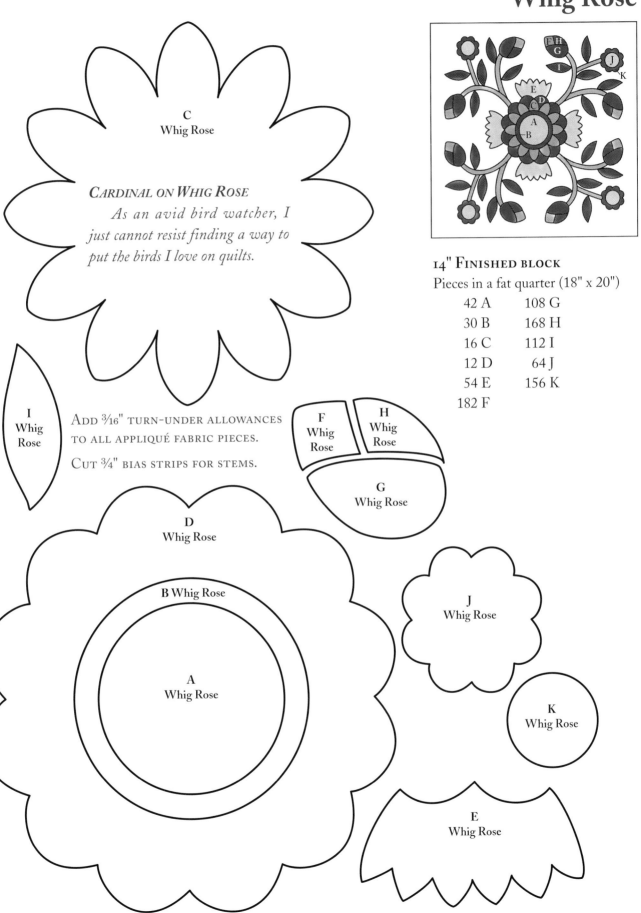

C
Whig Rose

CARDINAL ON WHIG ROSE
As an avid bird watcher, I just cannot resist finding a way to put the birds I love on quilts.

14" FINISHED BLOCK
Pieces in a fat quarter (18" x 20")

42 A	108 G
30 B	168 H
16 C	112 I
12 D	64 J
54 E	156 K
182 F	

I
Whig Rose

ADD ³⁄₁₆" TURN-UNDER ALLOWANCES TO ALL APPLIQUÉ FABRIC PIECES.

CUT ³⁄₄" BIAS STRIPS FOR STEMS.

F
Whig Rose

H
Whig Rose

G
Whig Rose

D
Whig Rose

B Whig Rose

A
Whig Rose

J
Whig Rose

K
Whig Rose

E
Whig Rose

Fence Row Star

Fence Row Star

A
Fence Row Star

D
Fence Row Star

Rotary cut ⊠ 7½" x 7½"

B
Fence
Row
Star

C
Fence Row Star

Rotary cut ▢ 4⅞" x 4⅞"

15" FINISHED BLOCK
Pieces in a fat quarter (18" x 20")

55 A
168 B
12 C
16 D

FENCE ROW STAR

If you notice, I put a bluebird on the fence. I consider the bluebird to be a "fence row star". They always sit on fences as if they were built only for them.

ADD ¼" SEAM ALLOWANCES TO YOUR TEMPLATES BEFORE CUTTING.

Double Irish Chain with Shamrocks

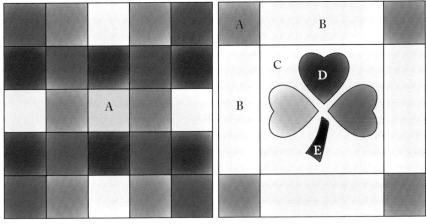

Double Irish Chain

10" **Finished block**

Pieces in a yard (36" x 40")

224 A

84 B

30 C

Pieces in a fat quarter (18" x 20")

36 D

70 E

Block 1   *Block 2*

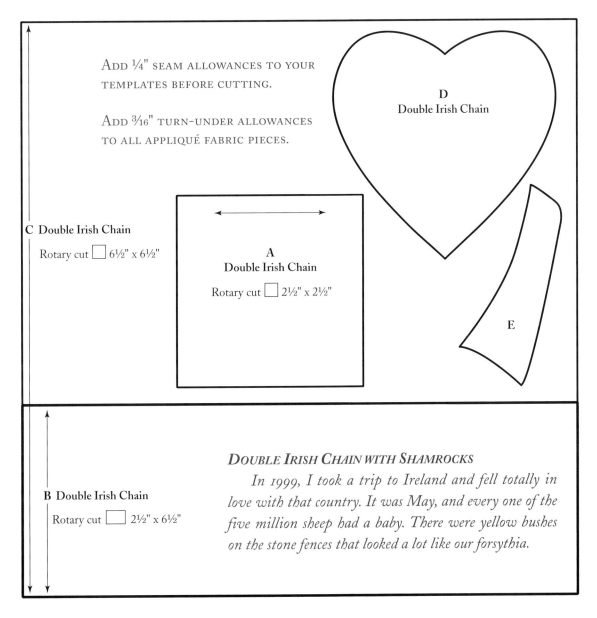

Add ¼" seam allowances to your templates before cutting.

Add ³/₁₆" turn-under allowances to all appliqué fabric pieces.

D
Double Irish Chain

C Double Irish Chain

Rotary cut ☐ 6½" x 6½"

A
Double Irish Chain

Rotary cut ☐ 2½" x 2½"

E

B Double Irish Chain

Rotary cut ☐ 2½" x 6½"

DOUBLE IRISH CHAIN WITH SHAMROCKS

In 1999, I took a trip to Ireland and fell totally in love with that country. It was May, and every one of the five million sheep had a baby. There were yellow bushes on the stone fences that looked a lot like our forsythia.

Field and Stream

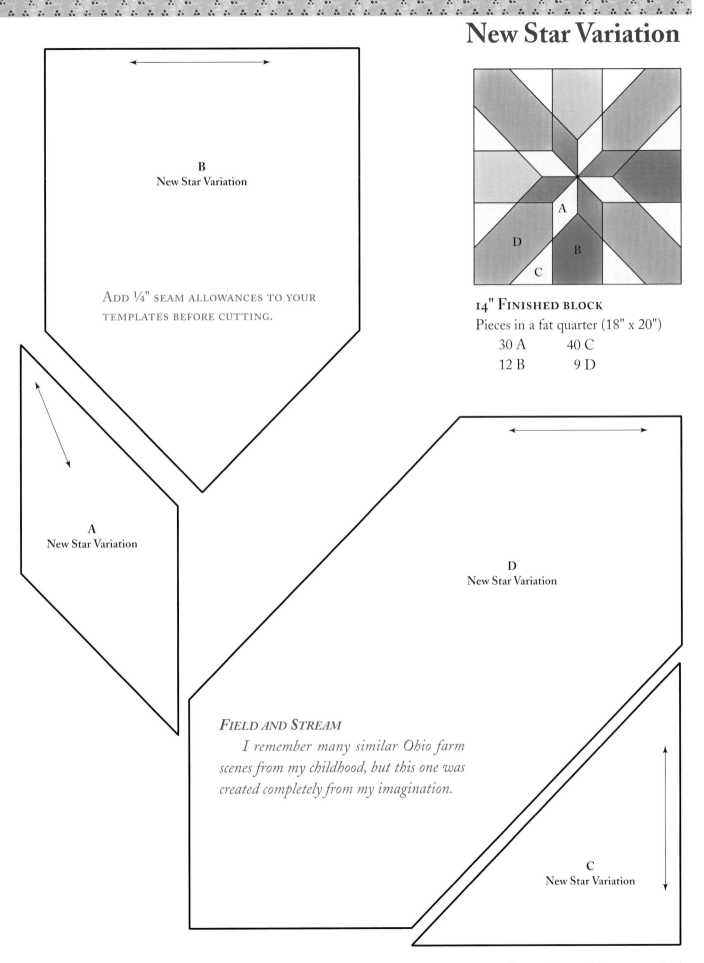

B
New Star Variation

Add ¼" seam allowances to your templates before cutting.

14" Finished block
Pieces in a fat quarter (18" x 20")

30 A	40 C
12 B	9 D

A
New Star Variation

D
New Star Variation

FIELD AND STREAM
I remember many similar Ohio farm scenes from my childhood, but this one was created completely from my imagination.

C
New Star Variation

Democratic Rose

I love appliqué patterns and often paint only the flowers instead of the whole quilt. These paintings provide a great way for me to experiment with colors.

Democratic Rose

14" Finished block
Pieces in a fat quarter (18" x 20")

156 A	112 F
42 B	144 G
16 C	130 H
20 D	140 I
132 E	

C
Democratic Rose

Add ³⁄₁₆" turn-under allowances to all appliqué fabric pieces.

Cut ¾" bias strips for stems.

D
Democratic Rose

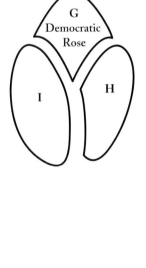

G
Democratic Rose

I

H

B
Democratic Rose

A
Democratic Rose

F

E
Democratic Rose

Sunny Lane

Sunny Lane

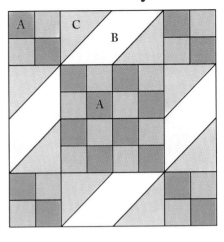

ADD ¼" SEAM ALLOWANCES TO YOUR
TEMPLATES BEFORE CUTTING.

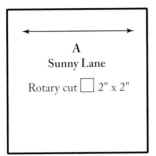

A
Sunny Lane

Rotary cut ☐ 2" x 2"

12" FINISHED BLOCK
Pieces in a fat quarter (18" x 20")
 90 A
 16 B
 40 C

SUNNY LANE

*My father and grandfather would send me to bring the cows in
to be milked, and I walked down a sunny lane just like this one.*

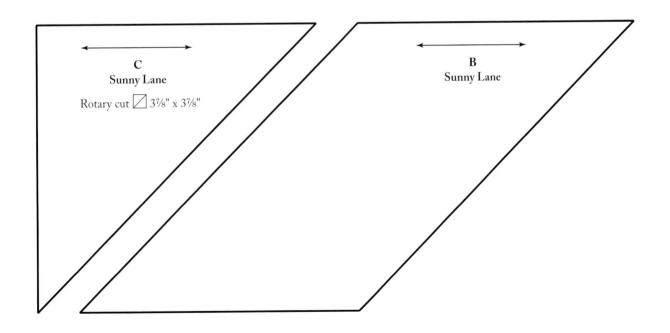

C
Sunny Lane

Rotary cut ◺ 3⅞" x 3⅞"

B
Sunny Lane

Rose of Sharon

This was one of my earliest quilt paintings. I grew up in a family that collects antiques, and my mother has an antique quilt collection, hence my first quilt paintings were usually of these traditional patterns.

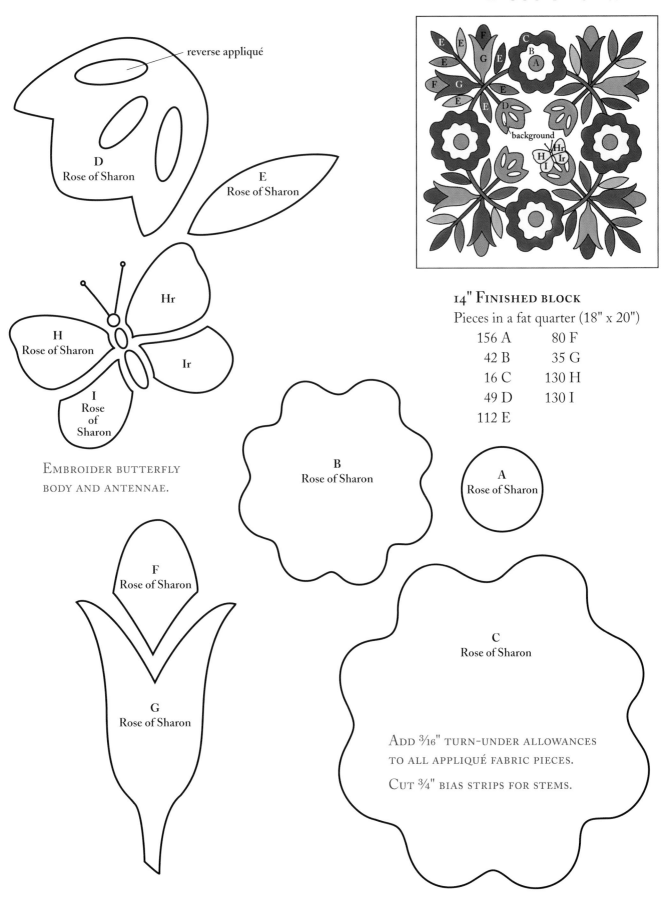

Rose of Sharon

reverse appliqué

D
Rose of Sharon

E
Rose of Sharon

Hr

H
Rose of Sharon

Ir

I
Rose of Sharon

EMBROIDER BUTTERFLY
BODY AND ANTENNAE.

B
Rose of Sharon

A
Rose of Sharon

14" FINISHED BLOCK

Pieces in a fat quarter (18" x 20")

156 A	80 F
42 B	35 G
16 C	130 H
49 D	130 I
112 E	

F
Rose of Sharon

G
Rose of Sharon

C
Rose of Sharon

ADD ³⁄₁₆" TURN-UNDER ALLOWANCES
TO ALL APPLIQUÉ FABRIC PIECES.

CUT ³⁄₄" BIAS STRIPS FOR STEMS.

Corn and Beans

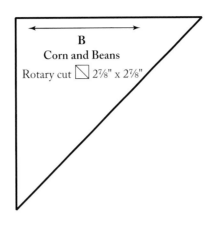

B
Corn and Beans

Rotary cut ⬜ 2⅞" x 2⅞"

Corn and Beans

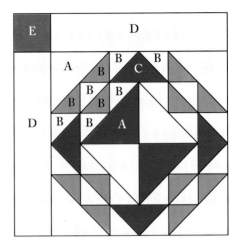

E **D**

E

D
D

B B
A
B C
B
B B
B B
A
B B

12" FINISHED BLOCK

Pieces in a yard (36" x 40")

 112 A

 312 B

 168 C

 42 D (sashing)

Pieces in a fat quarter (18" x 20")

 56 E (cornerstones)

place on fold

D
Corn and Beans

Rotary cut ⬜ 2½" x 12½"

CORN AND BEANS

On my family's farm, we raised field corn and soybeans, which I could see outside my bedroom window when I was a child.

ADD ¼" SEAM ALLOWANCES TO YOUR TEMPLATES BEFORE CUTTING.

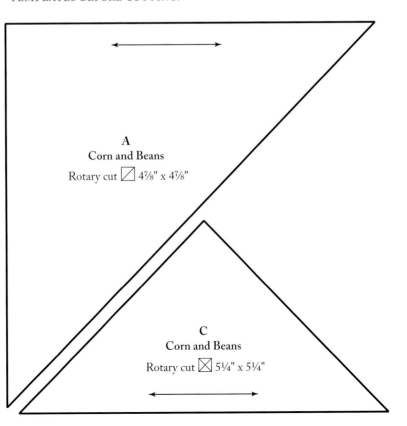

A
Corn and Beans

Rotary cut ◩ 4⅞" x 4⅞"

C
Corn and Beans

Rotary cut ⊠ 5¼" x 5¼"

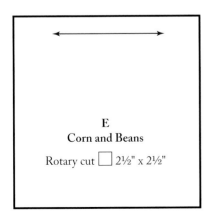

E
Corn and Beans

Rotary cut ⬜ 2½" x 2½"

Bluebirds on Wild Rose Wreath

Wild Rose Wreath

BLUEBIRDS ON *WILD ROSE WREATH

This is one of my many bird paintings. I go bird watching often and feed the birds outside my kitchen window. The bluebirds often rest on the rose bushes, which gave me the idea for this painting.

ADD ³⁄₁₆" TURN-UNDER ALLOWANCES
TO ALL APPLIQUÉ FABRIC PIECES.

CUT ¾" BIAS STRIPS FOR STEMS.

14" FINISHED BLOCK

Pieces in a fat quarter (18" x 20")

156 A	224 E
64 B	88 F
90 C	88 G
100 D	

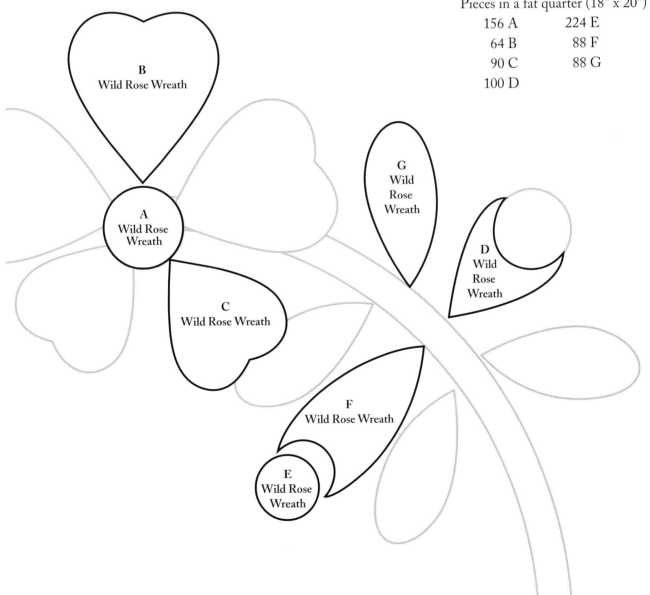

B
Wild Rose Wreath

A
Wild Rose
Wreath

C
Wild Rose Wreath

G
Wild
Rose
Wreath

D
Wild
Rose
Wreath

F
Wild Rose Wreath

E
Wild Rose
Wreath

Kentucky Crossroads

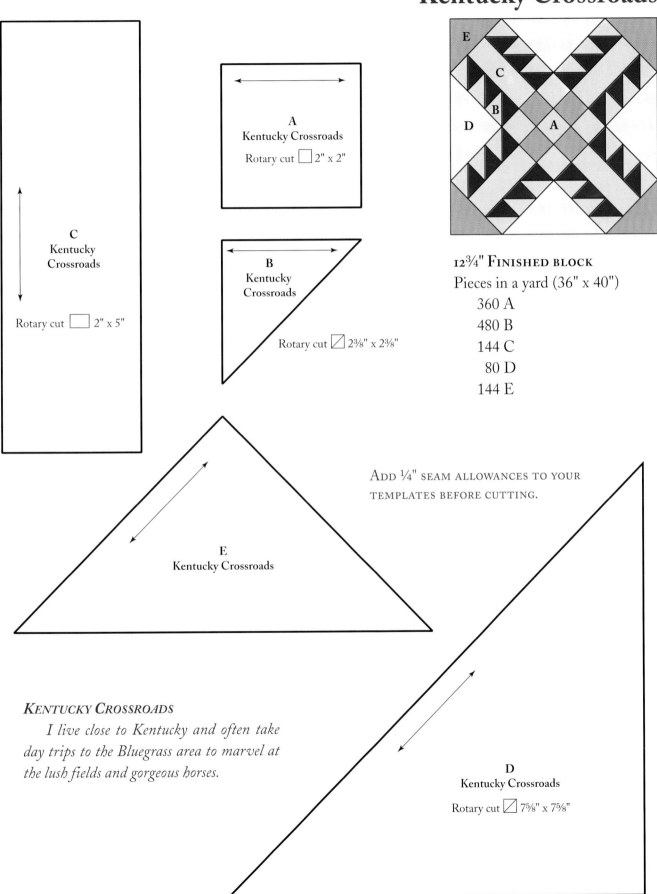

Kentucky Crossroads

A
Kentucky Crossroads

Rotary cut ☐ 2" x 2"

C
Kentucky
Crossroads

Rotary cut ☐ 2" x 5"

B
Kentucky
Crossroads

Rotary cut ◹ 2⅜" x 2⅜"

12¾" FINISHED BLOCK
Pieces in a yard (36" x 40")
360 A
480 B
144 C
80 D
144 E

ADD ¼" SEAM ALLOWANCES TO YOUR
TEMPLATES BEFORE CUTTING.

E
Kentucky Crossroads

D
Kentucky Crossroads

Rotary cut ◹ 7⅝" x 7⅝"

KENTUCKY CROSSROADS

I live close to Kentucky and often take day trips to the Bluegrass area to marvel at the lush fields and gorgeous horses.

Cosmos

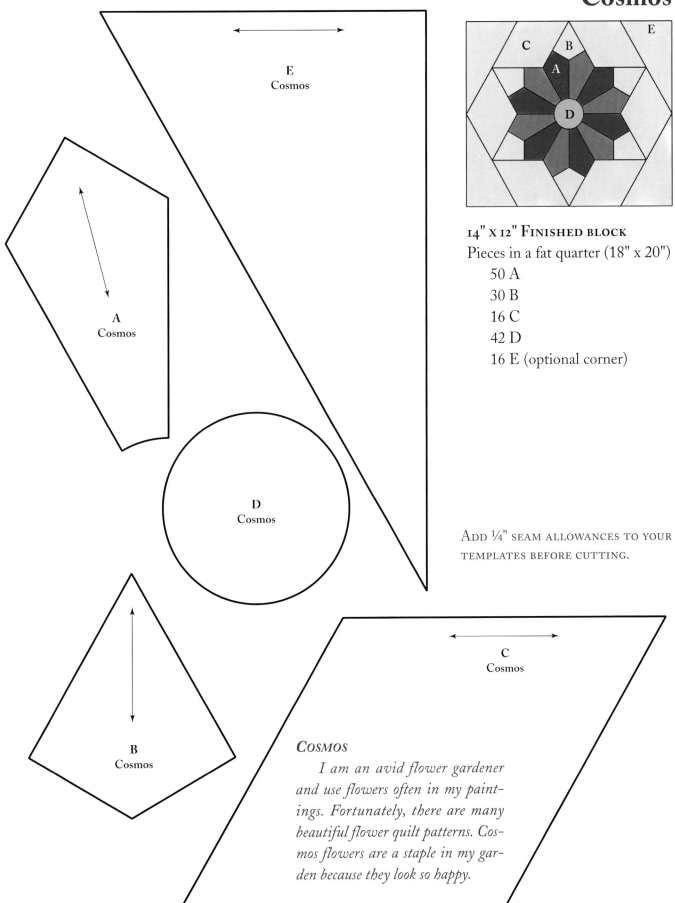

Cosmos

14" x 12" Finished block

Pieces in a fat quarter (18" x 20")

    50 A

    30 B

    16 C

    42 D

    16 E (optional corner)

Add ¼" seam allowances to your templates before cutting.

E
Cosmos

A
Cosmos

D
Cosmos

C
Cosmos

B
Cosmos

COSMOS

    I am an avid flower gardener and use flowers often in my paintings. Fortunately, there are many beautiful flower quilt patterns. Cosmos flowers are a staple in my garden because they look so happy.

Swing in the Middle

Swing in the Middle

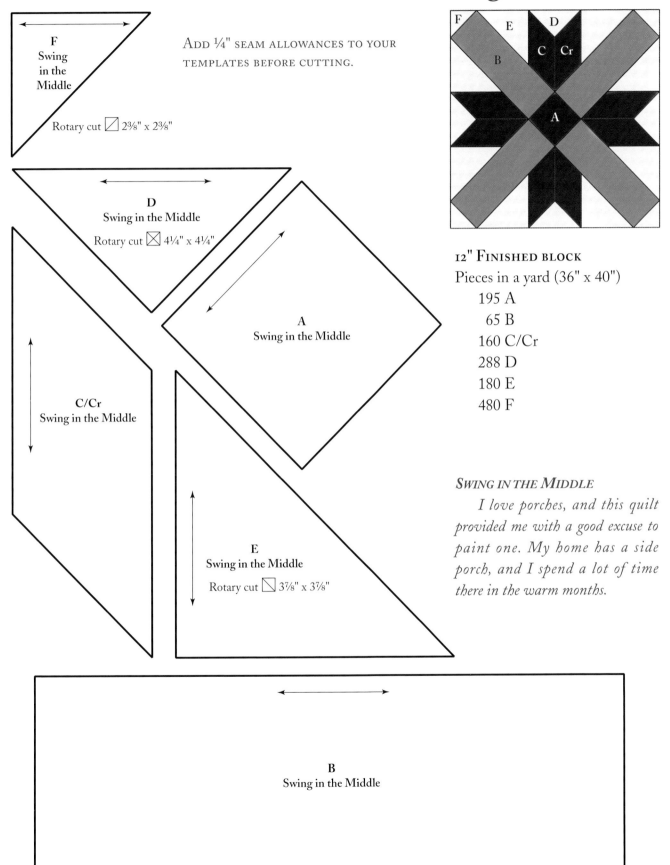

F
Swing
in the
Middle

Rotary cut ◻ 2⅜" x 2⅜"

Add ¼" seam allowances to your templates before cutting.

D
Swing in the Middle

Rotary cut ⊠ 4¼" x 4¼"

A
Swing in the Middle

C/Cr
Swing in the Middle

E
Swing in the Middle

Rotary cut ◻ 3⅞" x 3⅞"

B
Swing in the Middle

12" Finished block
Pieces in a yard (36" x 40")
- 195 A
- 65 B
- 160 C/Cr
- 288 D
- 180 E
- 480 F

Swing in the Middle

I love porches, and this quilt provided me with a good excuse to paint one. My home has a side porch, and I spend a lot of time there in the warm months.

Hummingbirds

Hummingbirds

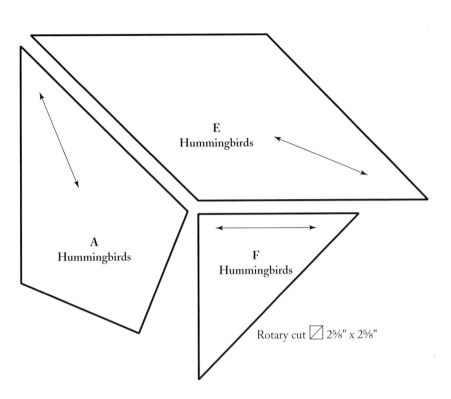

E
Hummingbirds

A
Hummingbirds

F
Hummingbirds

Rotary cut ◩ 2⅝" x 2⅝"

ADD ¼" SEAM ALLOWANCES TO YOUR
TEMPLATES BEFORE CUTTING.

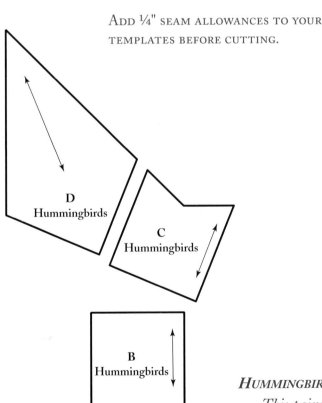

D
Hummingbirds

C
Hummingbirds

B
Hummingbirds

Rotary cut ☐ 1½" x 1½"

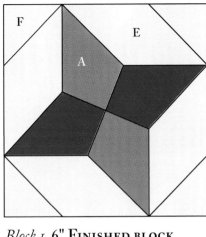

Block 1, 6" FINISHED BLOCK

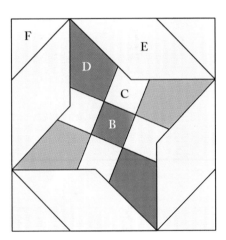

Block 2, 6" FINISHED BLOCK

Pieces in a fat quarter (18" x 20")
- 39 A
- 143 B
- 144 C
- 59 D
- 33 E
- 84 F (optional)

Use F if you want to make
blocks square.

HUMMINGBIRDS

*This painting incorporates my three loves, quilts, birds, and flowers.
There are two hummingbirds in this picture…I tried to hide one.*

Firefly

ADD ¼" SEAM ALLOWANCES TO YOUR
TEMPLATES BEFORE CUTTING.

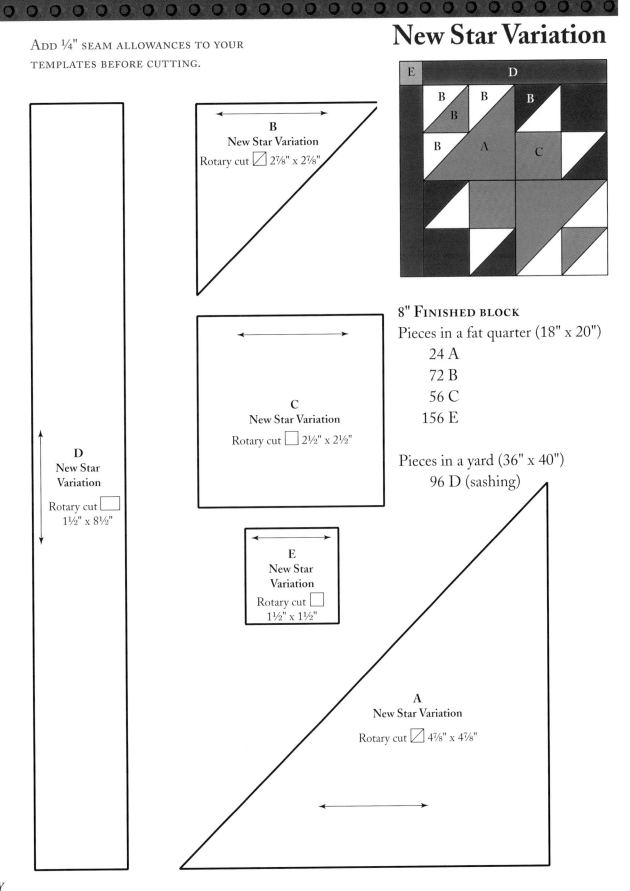

B
New Star Variation
Rotary cut ⬜ 2⅞" x 2⅞"

C
New Star Variation
Rotary cut ⬜ 2½" x 2½"

D
New Star
Variation
Rotary cut ⬜
1½" x 8½"

E
New Star
Variation
Rotary cut ⬜
1½" x 1½"

A
New Star Variation
Rotary cut ⬜ 4⅞" x 4⅞"

8" FINISHED BLOCK
Pieces in a fat quarter (18" x 20")

    24 A

    72 B

    56 C

    156 E

Pieces in a yard (36" x 40")

    96 D (sashing)

FIREFLY

   The paintings that are dearest to my heart are the ones that bring back childhood memories. This one recalls warm summer nights spent running around the yard with my brothers and sister, catching lightning bugs.

Fish

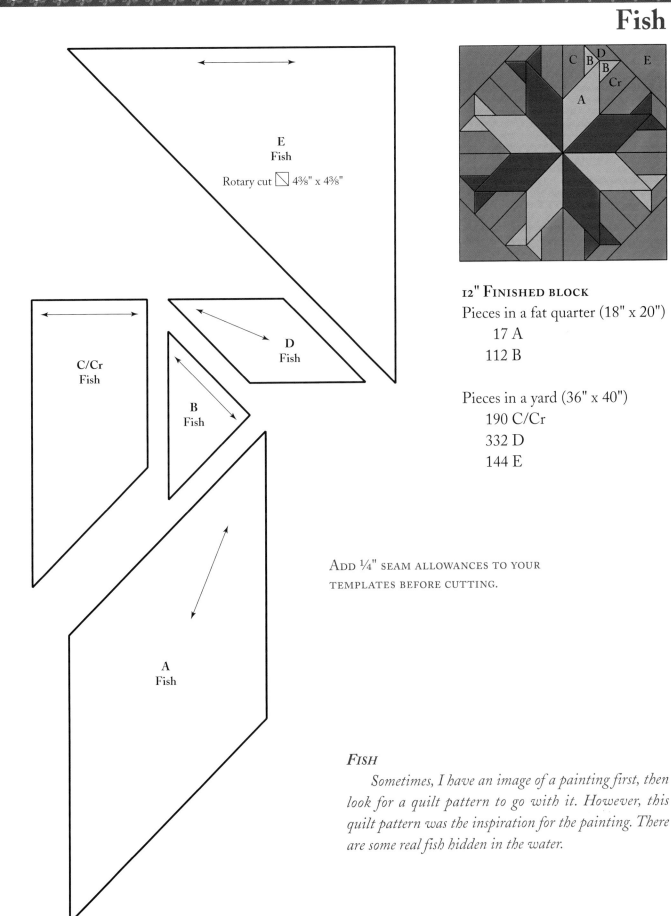

E
Fish

Rotary cut ◻ 4⅜" x 4⅜"

C/Cr
Fish

D
Fish

B
Fish

A
Fish

12" Finished block
Pieces in a fat quarter (18" x 20")
　　17 A
　　112 B

Pieces in a yard (36" x 40")
　　190 C/Cr
　　332 D
　　144 E

Add ¼" seam allowances to your templates before cutting.

Fish

Sometimes, I have an image of a painting first, then look for a quilt pattern to go with it. However, this quilt pattern was the inspiration for the painting. There are some real fish hidden in the water.

Palm Leaf

This simple, elegant quilt pattern makes me think of warm ocean breezes and clear blue skies, my dream vacation spot captured in paint.

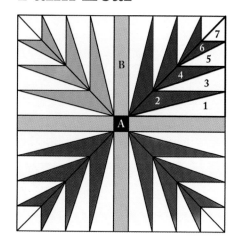

Palm Leaf

14" FINISHED BLOCK

Pieces in a fat quarter (18" x 20")

    156 A

    24 B

ADD ¼" SEAM ALLOWANCES TO PATTERNS A AND B AND THE OUTSIDE EDGE OF THE PAPER FOUNDATION PATTERN BEFORE CUTTING.

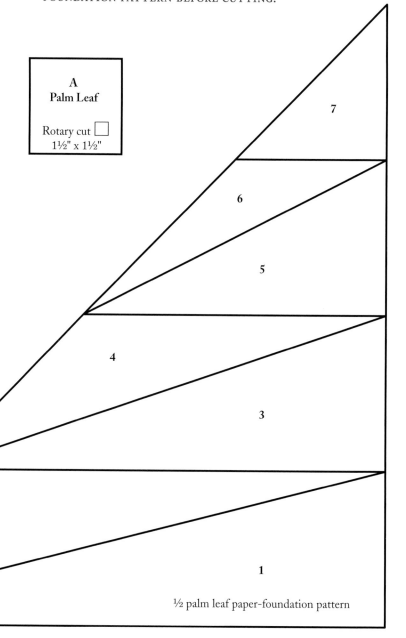

A
Palm Leaf

Rotary cut ☐
1½" x 1½"

½ palm leaf paper-foundation pattern

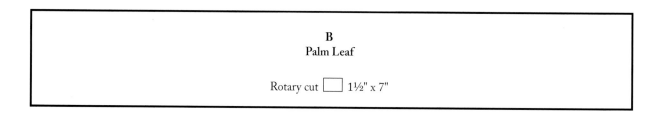

B
Palm Leaf

Rotary cut ☐ 1½" x 7"

Fourth of July

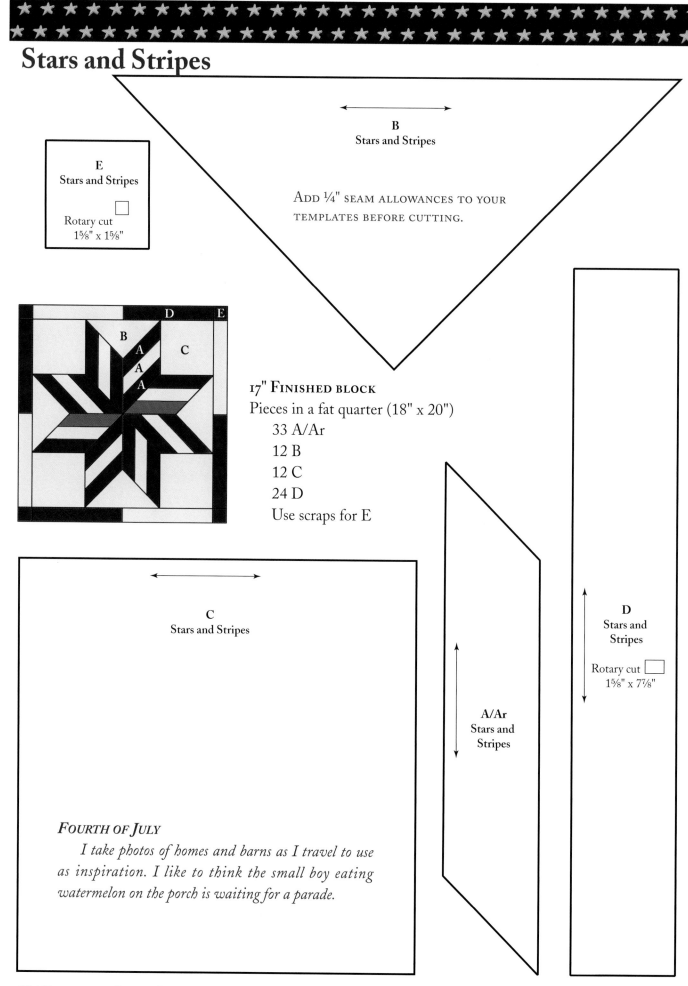

Stars and Stripes

E
Stars and Stripes

Rotary cut
1⅝" x 1⅝"

B
Stars and Stripes

ADD ¼" SEAM ALLOWANCES TO YOUR
TEMPLATES BEFORE CUTTING.

17" FINISHED BLOCK
Pieces in a fat quarter (18" x 20")
    33 A/Ar
    12 B
    12 C
    24 D
    Use scraps for E

C
Stars and Stripes

A/Ar
Stars and Stripes

D
Stars and
Stripes

Rotary cut
1⅝" x 7⅞"

FOURTH OF JULY

*I take photos of homes and barns as I travel to use
as inspiration. I like to think the small boy eating
watermelon on the porch is waiting for a parade.*

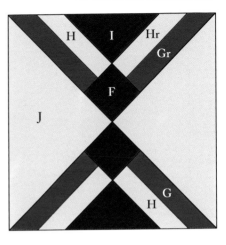

Firecrackers

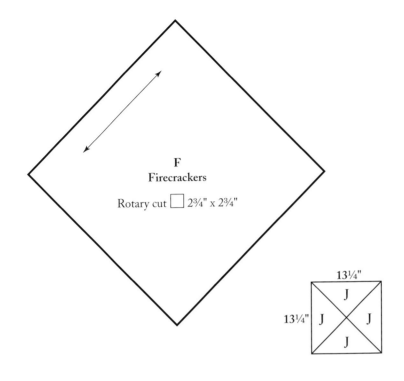

F
Firecrackers

Rotary cut ▢ 2¾" x 2¾"

13¼"

13¼"

| J |
| J | J |
| J |

12" FINISHED BLOCK

Pieces in a yard (36" x 40")

182 F	100 I
100 G/Gr	24 J
120 H/Hr	

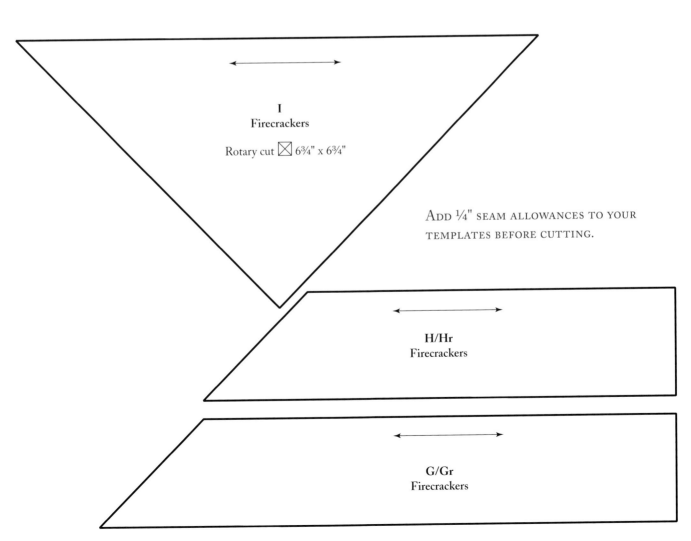

I
Firecrackers

Rotary cut ⊠ 6¾" x 6¾"

ADD ¼" SEAM ALLOWANCES TO YOUR TEMPLATES BEFORE CUTTING.

H/Hr
Firecrackers

G/Gr
Firecrackers

Sea Star

I envisioned a ship as the star of this quilt painting. Sunsets are very peaceful to paint, just as they are to watch.

Sea Star

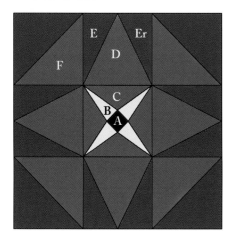

12" FINISHED BLOCK

Pieces in a fat quarter (18" x 20")

    156 A

     92 B

     40 C

     21 D

     36 E/Er

     24 F

ADD ¼" SEAM ALLOWANCES TO YOUR TEMPLATES BEFORE CUTTING.

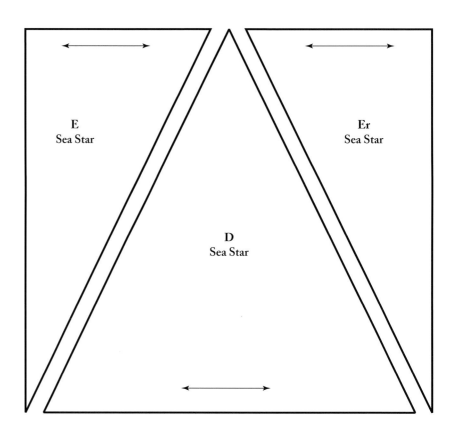

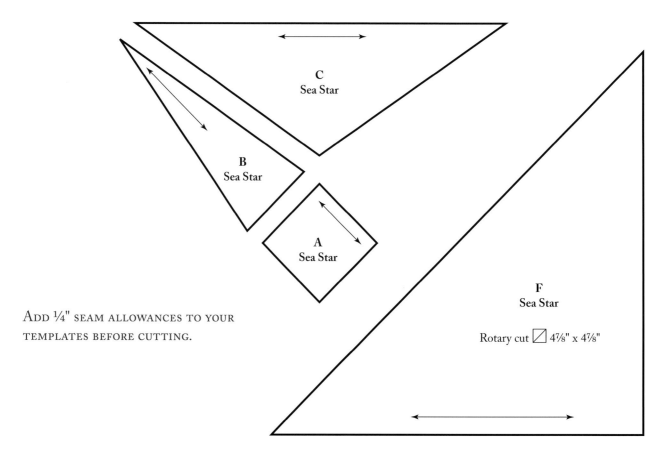

Grape Vine Wreath

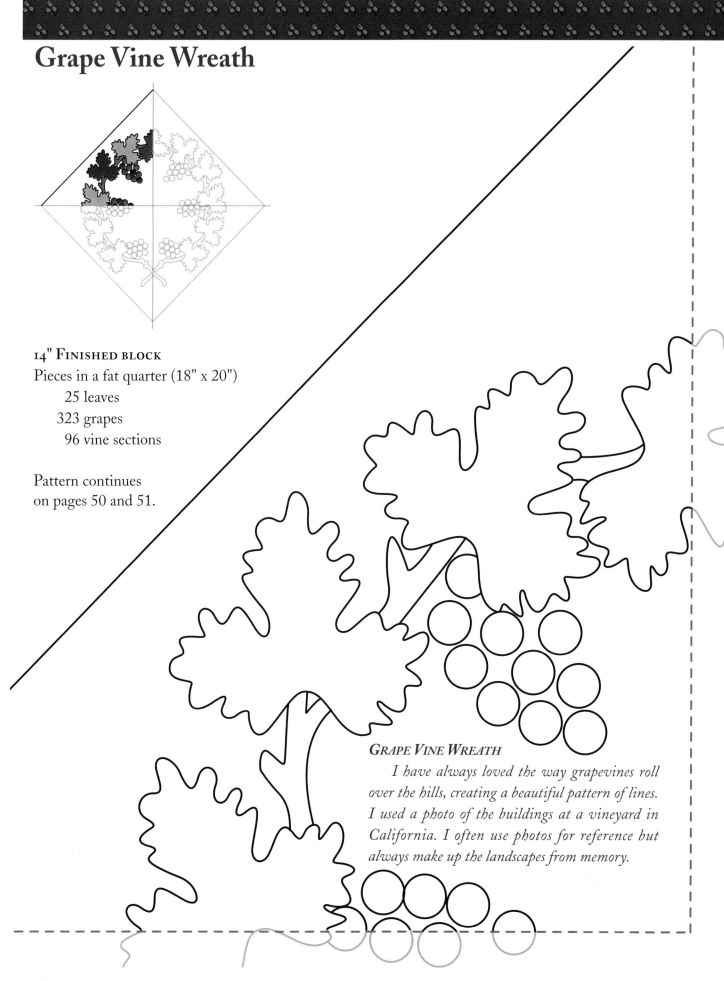

Grape Vine Wreath

14" FINISHED BLOCK
Pieces in a fat quarter (18" x 20")
    25 leaves
    323 grapes
    96 vine sections

Pattern continues
on pages 50 and 51.

GRAPE VINE WREATH
   I have always loved the way grapevines roll over the hills, creating a beautiful pattern of lines. I used a photo of the buildings at a vineyard in California. I often use photos for reference but always make up the landscapes from memory.

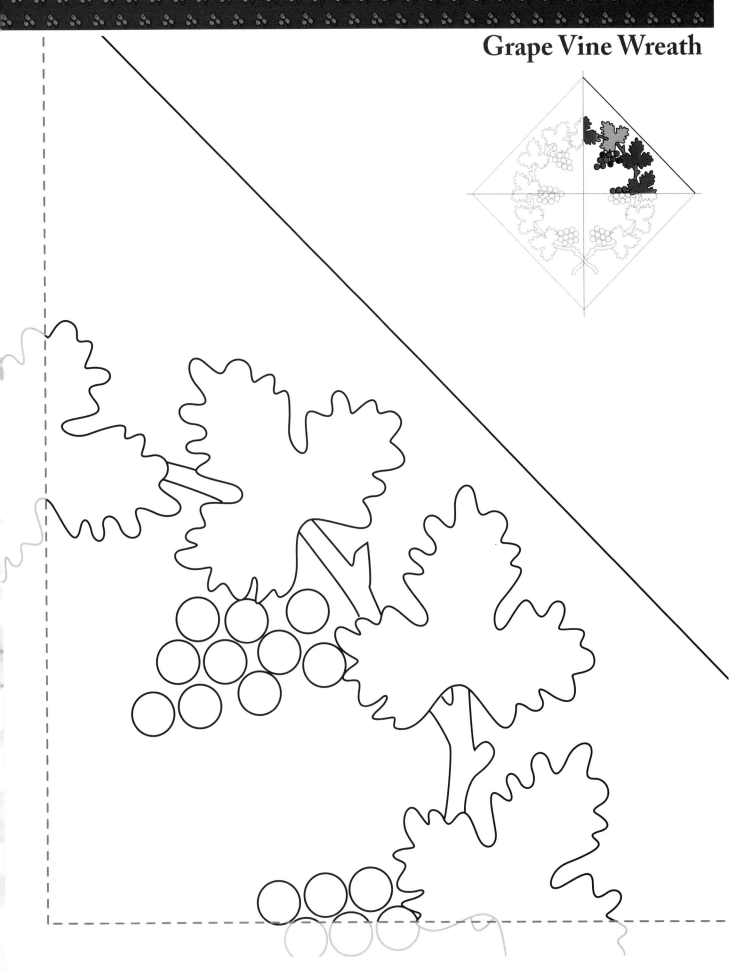

Grape Vine Wreath

Orange Basket

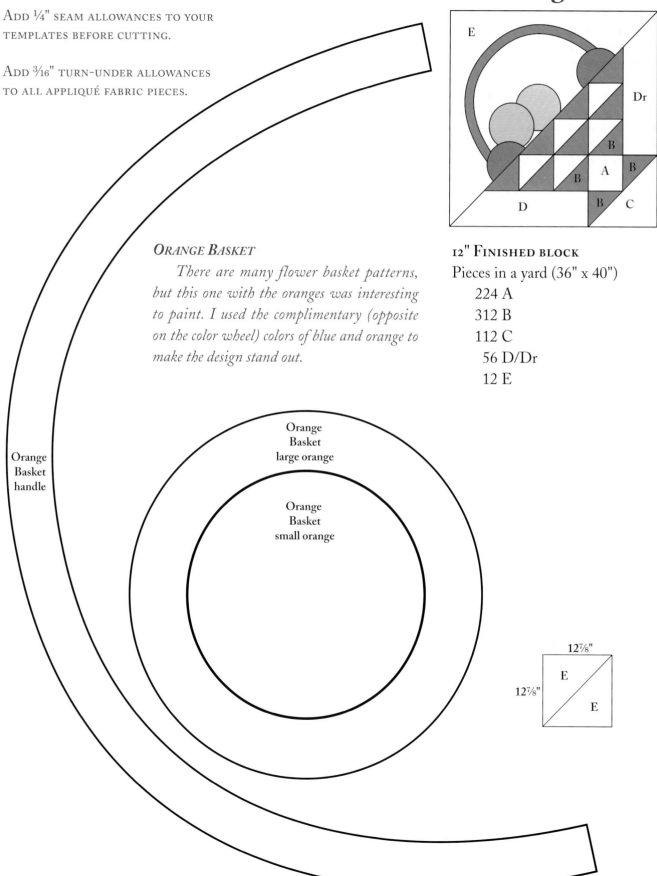

Orange Basket

Add ¼" seam allowances to your templates before cutting.

Add ³⁄₁₆" turn-under allowances to all appliqué fabric pieces.

ORANGE BASKET

There are many flower basket patterns, but this one with the oranges was interesting to paint. I used the complimentary (opposite on the color wheel) colors of blue and orange to make the design stand out.

12" Finished block

Pieces in a yard (36" x 40")

 224 A
 312 B
 112 C
  56 D/Dr
  12 E

Orange Basket handle

Orange Basket large orange

Orange Basket small orange

12⅞"

12⅞"

E

E

Orange Basket

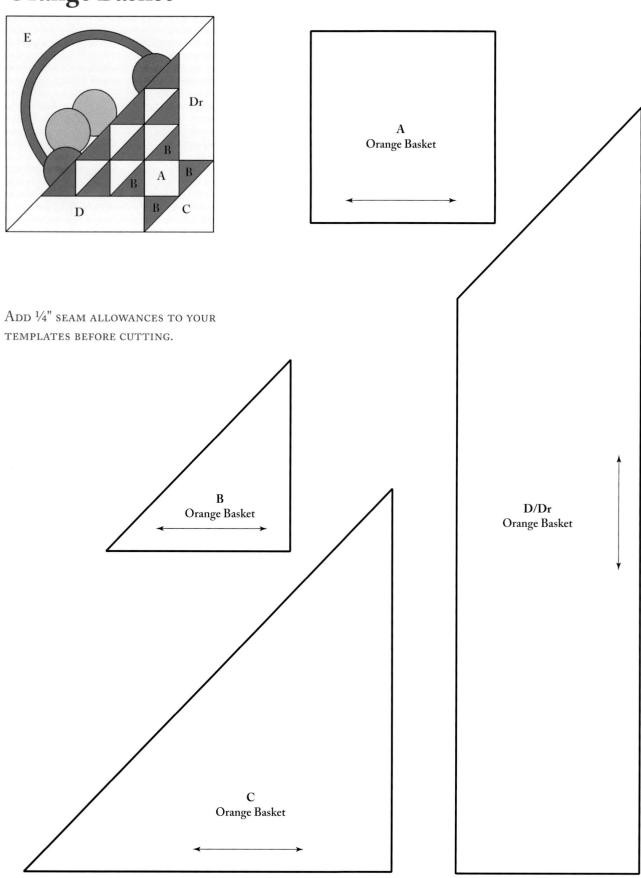

ADD ¼" SEAM ALLOWANCES TO YOUR TEMPLATES BEFORE CUTTING.

A
Orange Basket

B
Orange Basket

C
Orange Basket

D/Dr
Orange Basket

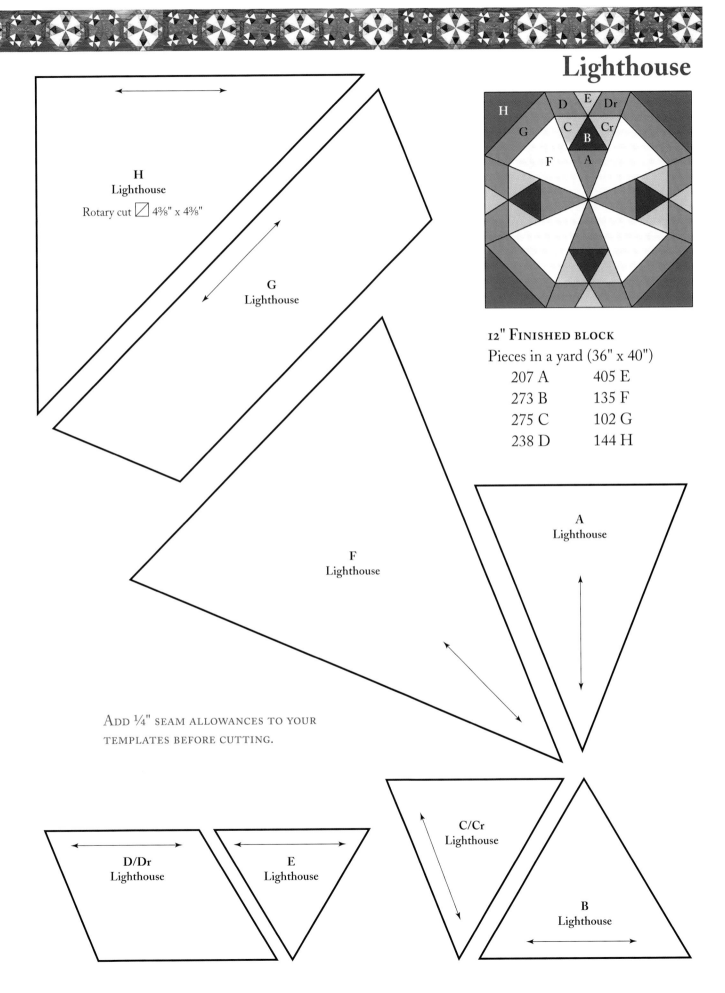

Lighthouse

H
Lighthouse

Rotary cut ⬜ 4⅜" x 4⅜"

G
Lighthouse

F
Lighthouse

ADD ¼" SEAM ALLOWANCES TO YOUR
TEMPLATES BEFORE CUTTING.

A
Lighthouse

12" FINISHED BLOCK

Pieces in a yard (36" x 40")

207 A	405 E
273 B	135 F
275 C	102 G
238 D	144 H

D/Dr
Lighthouse

E
Lighthouse

C/Cr
Lighthouse

B
Lighthouse

Lighthouse

Sunsets or evening light show up often in my work. I love the warm colors the sun gives off at that time of day. This painting looks rather simple, but it has 15 layers of paint in it.

Apple Tree

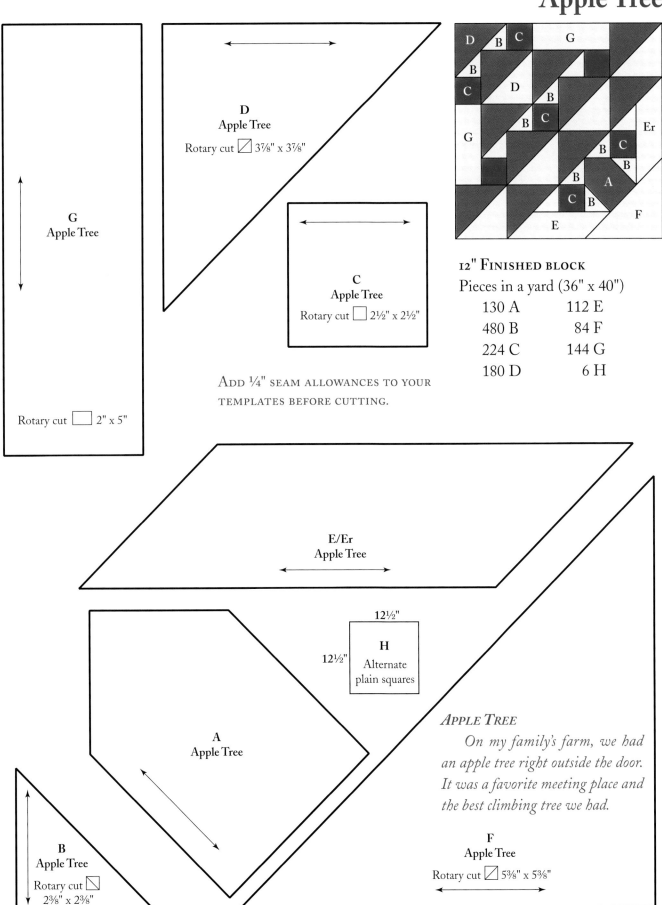

Apple Tree

G
Apple Tree

Rotary cut 2" x 5"

D
Apple Tree

Rotary cut ⬚ 3⅞" x 3⅞"

C
Apple Tree

Rotary cut ⬚ 2½" x 2½"

12" Finished block

Pieces in a yard (36" x 40")

130 A	112 E
480 B	84 F
224 C	144 G
180 D	6 H

ADD ¼" SEAM ALLOWANCES TO YOUR TEMPLATES BEFORE CUTTING.

E/Er
Apple Tree

12½"

H
Alternate plain squares

12½"

A
Apple Tree

APPLE TREE

On my family's farm, we had an apple tree right outside the door. It was a favorite meeting place and the best climbing tree we had.

B
Apple Tree

Rotary cut ⬚ 2⅜" x 2⅜"

F
Apple Tree

Rotary cut ⬚ 5⅜" x 5⅜"

Windmill

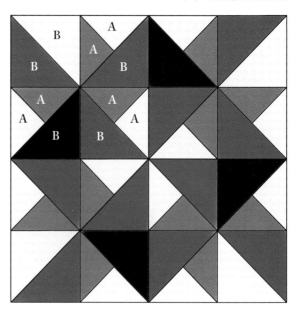

Windmill

ADD ¼" SEAM ALLOWANCES TO YOUR TEMPLATES BEFORE CUTTING.

12" FINISHED BLOCK
Pieces in a fat quarter (18" x 20")
    64 A
    40 B

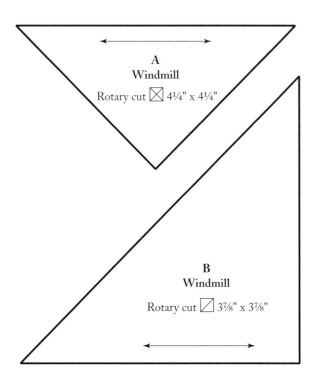

A
Windmill
Rotary cut ⊠ 4¼" x 4¼"

B
Windmill
Rotary cut ◹ 3⅞" x 3⅞"

WINDMILL

The Windmill pattern is appropriately named…you can almost feel the wind turning the blades.

Birds in the Air

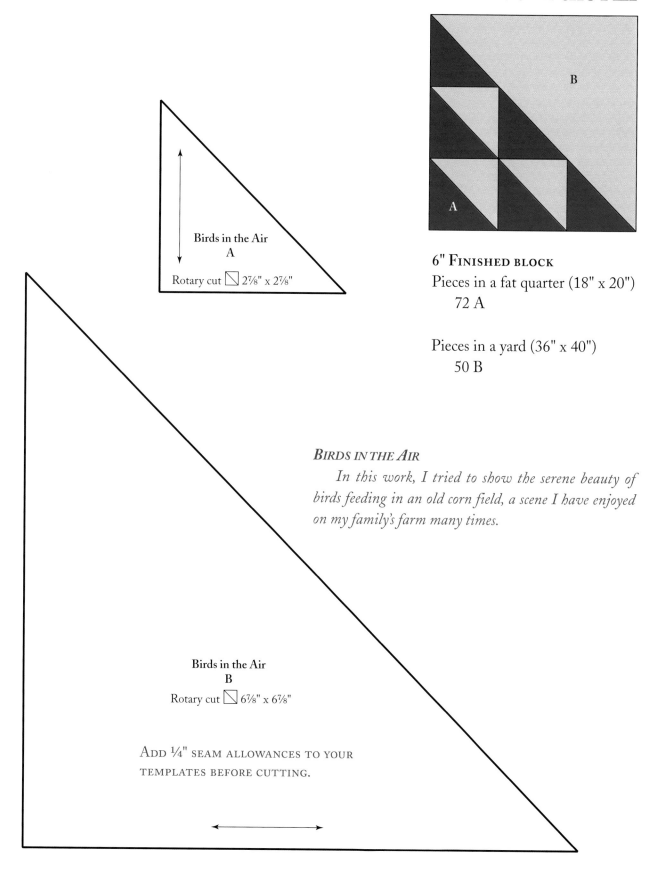

Birds in the Air

Birds in the Air
A

Rotary cut ◻ 2⅞" x 2⅞"

6" FINISHED BLOCK
Pieces in a fat quarter (18" x 20")
72 A

Pieces in a yard (36" x 40")
50 B

BIRDS IN THE AIR

In this work, I tried to show the serene beauty of birds feeding in an old corn field, a scene I have enjoyed on my family's farm many times.

Birds in the Air
B
Rotary cut ◻ 6⅞" x 6⅞"

ADD ¼" SEAM ALLOWANCES TO YOUR TEMPLATES BEFORE CUTTING.

Church Windows

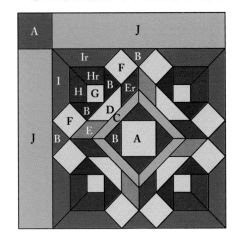

Church Windows

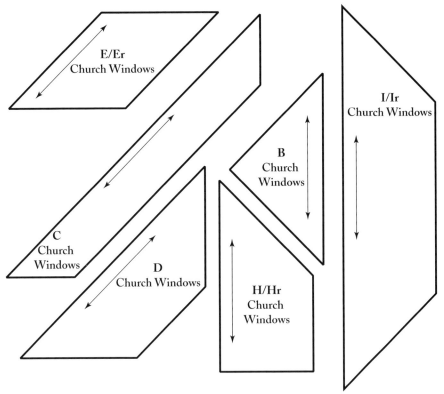

E/Er
Church Windows

C
Church
Windows

D
Church Windows

B
Church
Windows

H/Hr
Church
Windows

I/Ir
Church Windows

10" FINISHED BLOCK

Pieces in a fat quarter (18" x 20")

56 A

110 B

39 C

48 D

81 E/Er

90 F

143 G

66 H/Hr

33 I/Ir

Pieces in a yard (36" x 40")

42 J

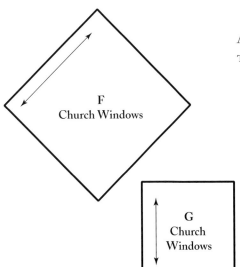

place on the fold

J
Church Windows

Rotary cut ☐ 2½" x 10½"

Church Windows
A

Rotary cut ☐ 2½" x 2½"

CHURCH WINDOWS

I often drive in the country and take pictures of little white churches, farm houses, and barns to use in my paintings. I use my imagination to create landscapes around buildings when I paint them.

F
Church Windows

G
Church
Windows

ADD ¼" SEAM ALLOWANCES TO YOUR TEMPLATES BEFORE CUTTING.

Flying Geese

Flying Geese

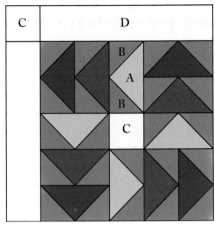

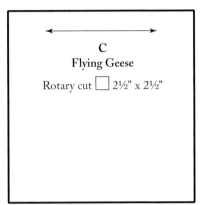

C
Flying Geese
Rotary cut ☐ 2½" x 2½"

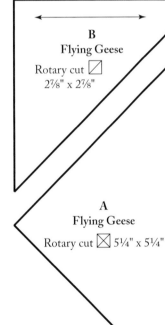

B
Flying Geese
Rotary cut ◺ 2⅞" x 2⅞"

A
Flying Geese
Rotary cut ⊠ 5¼" x 5¼"

D
Flying Geese
Rotary cut ☐ 2½" x 10½"

10" FINISHED BLOCK

Pieces in a fat quarter (18" x 20")
- 36 A
- 72 B
- 56 C

Pieces in a yard (36" x 40")
- 42 D (sashing)

FLYING GEESE

I chose snow geese to depict this pattern because I like the way they show up against the fields when they are feeding. This landscape could be anywhere in Indiana, which is only five miles from my home.

ADD ¼" SEAM ALLOWANCES TO YOUR TEMPLATES BEFORE CUTTING.

Steeplechase

The original inspiration for this quilt pattern was a steeplechase horse race, but I thought it would be nice to use church steeples instead.

Steeplechase

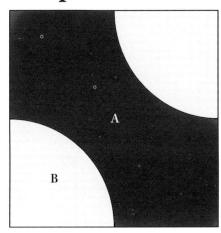

6" FINISHED BLOCK

Pieces in a fat quarter (18" x 20")

    6 A

    25 B

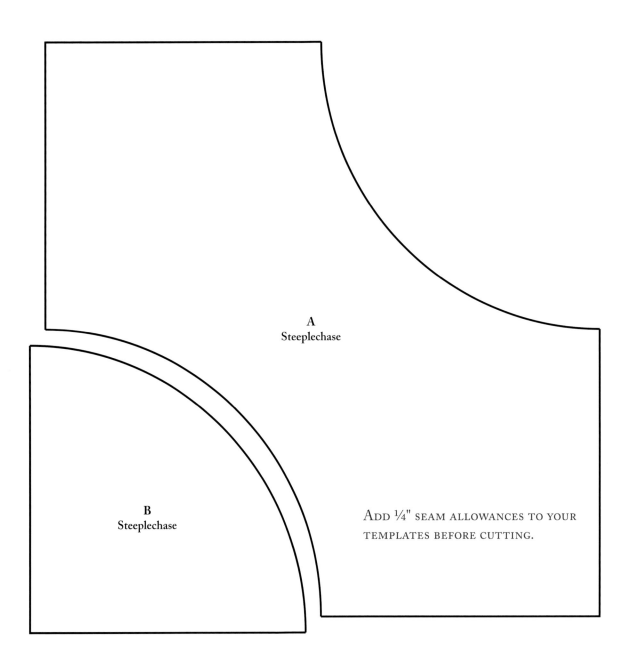

A
Steeplechase

B
Steeplechase

ADD ¼" SEAM ALLOWANCES TO YOUR
TEMPLATES BEFORE CUTTING.

Dogwood Blossom

This complicated but very beautiful quilt pattern was first published in Capper's Weekly in 1928.

Daffodil

This quilt integrates appliqué with a pieced quilt to produce a lovely pattern. I used the lamb with the daffodils to make it a spring season full of new life.

Grandmother's Flower Garden

This painting has been my all-time bestseller in print and notecards. I think we all want a porch and flower garden like this one, and many women have memories of this quilt pattern sewn by a loved one.

Ocean Waves

This was the most difficult painting I have ever attempted. Getting the perspective right in the foam and sand took forever, but it was worth the effort.

Oregon Trail

This quilt has many names: Drunkard's Path, Stone in the Road, Road to Dublin, Crooked Path, Pumpkin Vine, and several more.

Snow Crystals

The shape of the snowflake is the original inspiration for this quilt. The pattern was first published by the Kansas City Star, circa 1930.

Bibliography

I thank the authors of the following books for their help in studying the quilt patterns I have selected to paint.

Beyer, Jinny. *The Quilter's Album of Blocks & Borders.* McLean, Va.: EPM Publications, 1986.

Brackman, Barbara. *Encyclopedia of Appliqué.* McLean, Va.: EPM Publications, 1993.

——. *Encyclopedia of Pieced Quilt Patterns.* Paducah, Ky.: American Quilter's Society, 1993.

Davis, Nancy. *Maryland Historical Society. The Baltimore Album Quilt Tradition.* Tokyo, Japan: Kokusai Art, 1999.

Hall, Carrie and Rose Kretsinger. *The Romance of the Patchwork Quilt.* New York: Dover Publishing, 1963.

Ickis, Margaret. *The Standard Book of Quilt Making and Collecting.* New York: Dover Publishing, 1949.

Orlofsky, Patsy and Myron Orlofsky. *Quilts in America.* New York: McGraw-Hill, 1974.

Pellman, Rachel and Kenneth Pellman. *The Treasury of Amish Quilts.* Intercourse, Pa.: Good Books, 1990.

My Family's Farm House

This is my family's dairy farm in Oxford, Ohio. It has been in our family for seven generations, since 1811. I now live 40 minutes away and visit often. It is a huge source of strength and ideas for me.

Meet the Author

Growing up on her family's dairy farm in Oxford, Ohio, Rebecca acquired a love of country life and all things related, including quilting. She first learned about quilts from her mother, who made and collected them.

Rebecca has always loved to paint, and she knew from an early age that she wanted to be an artist. She received her art training from Ohio University in Athens, Ohio, and Miami University in Oxford, Ohio, and has pursued a painting career ever since.

Around 1994, having been a quilter for several years, she started to include quilts in her landscape paintings. The first of these depicts a quilt hanging on a clothesline in the foreground and a farm landscape in the background. Rebecca says, "This one painting received a lot of attention at an art show I attended, so I wanted to find out all I could about quilts." After that, she spent many hours reading quilt books and going to quilt shows to learn the patterns and their histories so she could create authentic quilts for her paintings.

Rebecca's beautiful paintings are available as notecards and limited edition prints. You can visit her website at www.barkerquiltscapes.com.

Other AQS Books

This is only a small selection of the books available from the American Quilter's Society. AQS books are known worldwide for timely topics, clear writing, beautiful color photos, and accurate illustrations and patterns. The following books are available from your local bookseller, quilt shop, or public library.

#6212   us$25.95

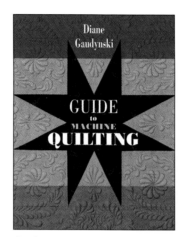

#6070   us$24.95

#6076   us$21.95

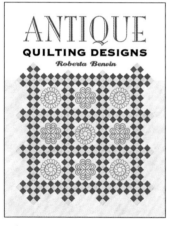

#5849   us$21.95

#5753   us$18.95

#6001   us$21.95

#6009   us$19.95

#4957   us$34.95

#5972   us$16.95

Look for these books nationally or call 1-800-626-5420